THE GOOD LION

by Beryl Markham

Adapted and Illustrated by Don Brown

HOUGHTON MIFFLIN COMPANY • BOSTON 2005

For Aunt Rita
who knows something of cats.

Illustrations and compilation of text © 2005 Don Brown
Text adapted from "He Was a Good Lion" from *West with the Night* by Beryl Markham.
Copyright © 1942, 1983 by Beryl Markham. Reproduced by arrangement with
North Point Press, a division of Farrar, Straus and Giroux, LLC.

www.houghtonmifflinbooks.com

The text of this book is set in 15-point ITC Cheltenham Book.
The illustrations are pencil and watercolor on paper.
Book design by Carol Goldenberg

Library of Congress Cataloging-in-Publication Data is on file.

LCCN 2004025121
ISBN-13: 978-0618-56306-7

Manufactured in Singapore
TWP 10 9 8 7 6 5 4 3 2 1

MY FATHER AND I SETTLED IN EAST AFRICA IN 1906. Africa was green hills, cool water, and bright mornings. It was generous in its harshness and favors, yielding nothing but offering much to people of all races. And it was where, as a small girl, I was eaten by a lion.

beryl

THERE WAS A PLACE CALLED Elkington Farm, near Nairobi on the edge of the Kikuyu Reserve. My father and I rode there from town, and along the way he told me about Africa.

He told me about the Masai, the Kikuyu, and the Murani tribes, and about their great leaders. I knew Murani hunters, and their life seemed much greater fun than my own—from them I learned about the wildebeest and antelope, leopard and buffalo, and the snake that crawls and the snake that climbs.

Often, my father spoke of lions.

"Lions are more intelligent than some men," he said, "and more courageous than most. You can always trust a lion to be exactly what he is, and never anything else.

"Except," he added, "that lion of Elkington's!"

Paddy, the Elkington lion, was tame. He wandered the fields and pastures without worry or care, like an emperor a-stroll in the gardens of his court. He was fed and had grown to full size, tawny, black-maned, and muscular. At night you could hear him roar when he was hungry, when he was sad, or when he just felt like roaring. This was the song of Paddy.

So Paddy ate, slept, and roared, and perhaps he sometimes dreamed, but he never left Elkington's.

"I'm always careful of him," I said to my father, "but he's really harmless. I've seen Mrs. Elkington stroke him."

"A tame lion is an unnatural lion," my father said, "and whatever is unnatural is untrustworthy."

Finally we reached the Elkington farm, where a thousand miles of Africa receded from its edge. On the farm was a nice house with a large verandah. There Father shared muffins, cake, and talk with the Elkingtons while I wandered toward the bush in search of small adventures.

I caught sight of Bishon Singh, a Sikh who tended the horses. Atop his head was a fantastic turban. There seemed so much of it and so little of Bishon Singh—was there one thousand yards of cloth in that turban? He raised his arm and greeted me in Swahili as I ran toward open country.

I was within yards of the Elkington lion before I saw him. He lay sprawled in the sun, his tail moving slowly, stroking the rough grass like a knotted rope end. He was not asleep; he was only still. He was rust red, like a strokable cat.

I stopped and he lifted his head.
He stared at me with yellow eyes.

I stared back, scuffling my bare toes in the dust, pursing my lips in a noiseless whistle—a very small girl who knew about lions. The lion raised himself and sighed. He sniffed the air.

I remembered not to run. Walking slowly, I began to sing a defiant song.

"*Kali coma Simba sisi,*" I sang. "Fierce like the lion are we!"

I went in a straight line past the lion, seeing his eyes shine, watching his tail beat time to the meter of my ditty. I cannot say there was any danger in his eyes. But he did not lie down again.

Singing still, I trotted toward a low hill that might, if I was lucky, have Cape gooseberry bushes on its slopes.

The country was gray-green and dry, and the sun lay on it closely, making the ground hot under my feet. There was no sound or wind.

Even the lion made no sound as he came swiftly behind me.

What followed was my scream that was barely a whisper, a blow that struck me to the ground, and teeth closing on my leg.

He roared, an immense roar that dissolved me in it. I lay still under the weight of Paddy's paws and tried not to be.

It was then that Bishon Singh's turban appeared over the edge of the hill.

Singh had seen Paddy go in the direction I had taken, and had decided to follow. A lion and a little girl are strange company, he thought.

Singh called for help and people raced to me. Mr. Elkington arrived with a mind to beat Paddy with a kiboko, but the lion was not in a mood to accept the punishment. Paddy rushed to Mr. Elkington, who fled to the top of a nearby tree.

Now there was an angry crowd where once was only a young girl and a lion.

That night, Paddy killed a horse, a bull, and a cow.

In the end, he was caught and caged, where he remained for many years. People stared at him and he stared back, and this went on until he was an old, old lion and his life ended.

Paddy had lived and died in ways not of his choosing. He was a good lion, and he had done what he could about being a tame lion. Who thinks it is fair to be judged by a single mistake?

I still have scars from his teeth and claws, but they are very small now and almost forgotten, and I do not begrudge him his moment.

End Note

BERYL MARKHAM was born in England in 1903, but moved to East Africa when she was three. She thrived in Africa and threw herself into the spirited, outdoor pursuits of her African playmates. At nineteen, she trained racehorses, a skill she learned from her father. Despite great success with horses, however, airplanes would capture her heart. She learned to fly and became a bush pilot, crisscrossing vast savannahs delivering mail and supplies, or spotting big game for safaris. In 1936, Beryl made the first solo east-to-west transatlantic flight.

Beryl's memoir of Africa and flying, *West with the Night*, was published in 1942 to great popular and critical success. And while there's controversy as to whether or not she actually wrote the book, it's a fantastic read. All of Beryl's adventures are amazing, but her childhood memories of East Africa are perhaps the most vivid. The story about Paddy is one such memory—a near tragedy—but Beryl finds only compassion and sympathy for the lion, and disagrees with punishing him for abiding his essential nature. It's an unforgettable story that upsets our notions of "tame" and "good" and makes this encounter truly remarkable.

Slugs in Love

by
Susan Pearson

illustrated by
Kevin O'Malley

Herbie   Marylou

Marshall Cavendish Children

E
PEA

Marshall Cavendish Corporation, 99 White Plains Road, Tarrytown, NY 10591
www.marshallcavendish.us

Library of Congress Cataloging-in-Publication Data
Pearson, Susan.
Slugs in love / by Susan Pearson ; illustrated by Kevin O'Malley.— 1st ed.
p. cm.
Summary: Marylou and Herbie, two garden slugs, write love poems in slime
to one another but have trouble actually meeting.
ISBN-13: 978-0-7614-5311-6
ISBN-10: 0-7614-5311-3
[1. Slugs (Mollusks)—Fiction. 2. Poetry—Fiction. 3. Love—Fiction.]
I. O'Malley, Kevin, 1961- ill. II. Title.
PZ8.3.P27473Slu 2006
[E]—dc22
2005027073

The text of this book is set in Garamond.
The illustrations were created using markers, colored pencils, and Photoshop.
Book design by Symon Chow

Printed in China
First edition
3 5 6 4 2

mc **Marshall Cavendish**
Children

For Rosemary and Dave
_S.P.

Marylou loved everything about Herbie—how his slime trail glistened in the dark, how he could stretch himself thin to squeeze inside the cellar window, how he always found the juiciest tomato. Though she never spoke a single word to him—she was too shy—she thought about Herbie every morning and every night and most of the hours in between.

On Monday, while she grazed in the strawberry patch, Herbie filled her mind and a love poem filled her heart. She wrote it in slime on the watering can.

The next morning, Herbie found it. He looked around. There were already at least sixty slugs in the garden. Which one, he wondered, was Marylou?

Herbie decided to send a message back. He wrote it on the garden hoe.

Marylou, which one are you?
Meet me here at half past two.
Yours truly,
      Herbie

But the gardener put the hoe
away in the barn, so Marylou never
saw Herbie's message.

On Tuesday, while Marylou was hiding from the sun in the ivy, she saw Herbie hiding under a stone, and a poem came immediately to mind. She wrote it on the wheelbarrow later that day.

The sun is shining all around.
It shines on field and tree.
But Herbie's safe beneath a rock—
I wish he'd think of me.
        Love,
        Marylou

"Marylou loves Herrrrrrrbie!" teased Jethro on Wednesday morning.

Herbie blushed. "Who *is* Marylou?" he asked, but Jethro didn't know either.

Herbie sent another message. This time he wrote it on a fence where it would stay put.

To Marylou:
You could make my life complete!
I'd love to meet someone so sweet.
Tell me where and I'll be there.
Sincerely,
Herbie

But that afternoon it rained and his letter washed away.

Even when Marylou was sleeping, poems to Herbie filled her dreams. She woke early and wrote another poem on the scarecrow.

"That Marylou is some poet!" said Sammy.

"Do you know her?" Herbie asked excitedly.

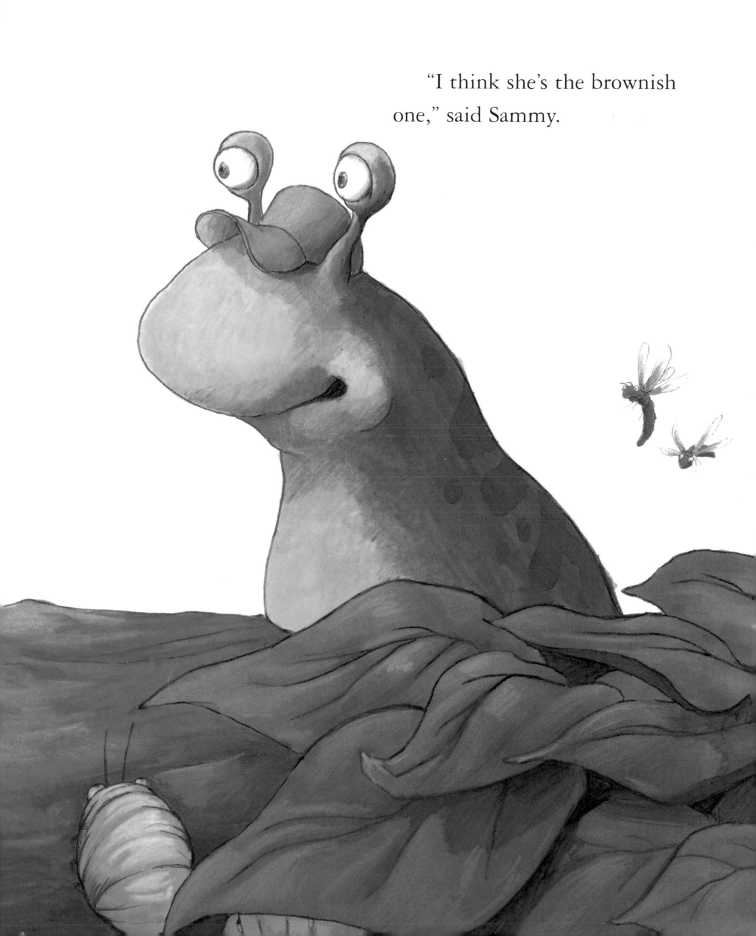

"I think she's the brownish one," said Sammy.

All day long Herbie searched for a brownish slug, but next to the brown dirt, they all looked a little brown. Herbie left another message on the watermelons.

Your poems make me happy.
Your poems make me glad.
But I can't find you, Marylou,
and that makes me feel sad!
Your friend,
Herbie

But Marylou was in the squash patch that day and didn't see Herbie's note. She left another poem behind on the zucchini.

Herbie was at his wit's end. He *had* been noticing her! Well, her poems anyway. And he'd asked everyone he could think of if they knew her.

"I think she's the greenish one," said Homer.

"I think she's the pinkish one," said Jodelle.

"Maybe she's the one who likes tomatoes," said Adelaide.

"*All* slugs like tomatoes!" said Herbie.

But Adelaide had given him an idea.

Herbie climbed to the top of the tallest tomato plant. On his way back down, he wrote a message.

Look at me!
I've climbed so high

that I can see
the world pass by:

mice and ants,
an old black shoe,

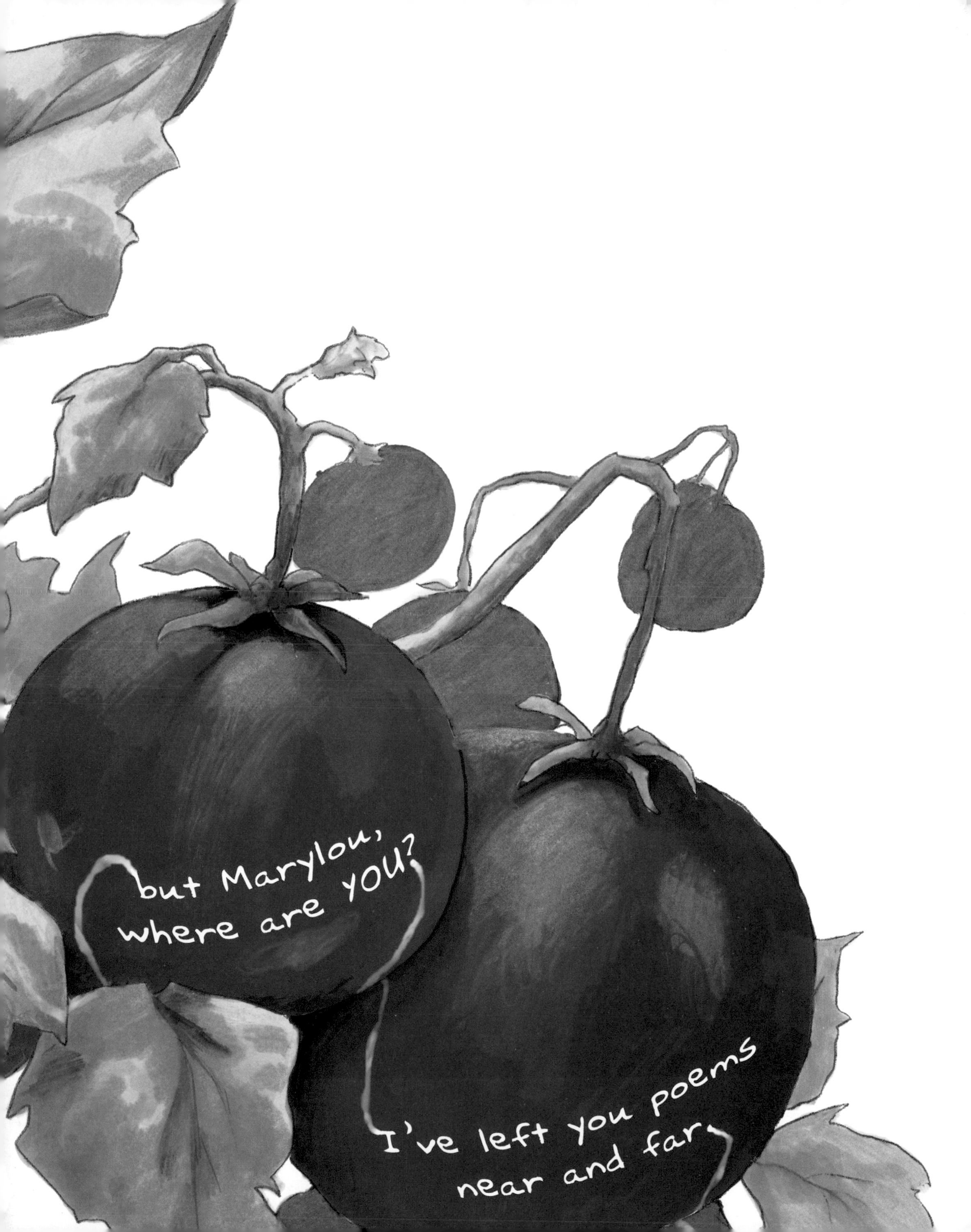

but Marylou,
where are YOU?

I've left you poems
near and far,

And that night, when Marylou went
out to snack on a tomato, she found
Herbie's message glistening in the
garden! What joy! What gladness!
What delight! Marylou could
hardly contain herself as she
hurried to the barn.

The next morning, the first thing Herbie saw was:

As always, when she saw Herbie, poetry filled
Marylou's head. She said:
    "Herbie, I am Marylou.
    We meet at last. How do you do?"
    Herbie was tongue-tied. Suddenly he felt shy.
But at last he blurted out:
    "I am fine.
    Will you be mine?"

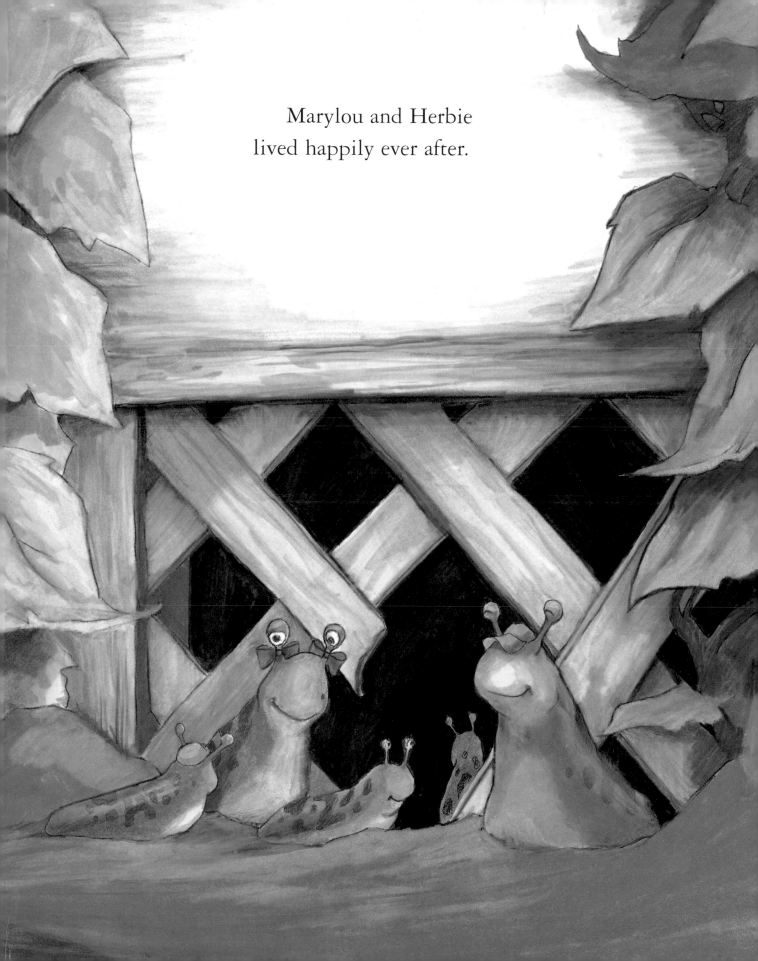

Marylou and Herbie
lived happily ever after.